OFFICIAL
HANDBOOK
FOR
VISITORS

Philadelphia

by

ROBERT H. WILSON

sponsored by

GIRARD BANK

Philadelphia

in cooperation with the

INDEPENDENCE HALL ASSOCIATION

THE HADLEY GROUP

CONTENTS

Ninth Printing

THIS BOOK WAS SET IN CASLON TYPE, AN EARLY TYPEFACE

USED BY BENJAMIN FRANKLIN.

Copyright © 1972, except maps, by Robert H. Wilson
Maps copyright © 1972 by Hammond Incorporated
Library of Congress Catalog Number 64-12384
ISBN 0-8437-4102-3
Printed in U.S.A.
Reproduction in whole or in part
prohibited without written permission
from the publisher.

WELCOME TO PHILADELPHIA

Among all the cities and sightseeing spots of America, Philadelphia offers a unique blend of the historic and the modern. Here in the midst of a great, vigorous 20th Century metropolis you find still carefully preserved the Colonial city where the American nation was born.

The city's headquarters for visitors is the attractive Tourist Center at Sixteenth Street and John F. Kennedy Boulevard — in Penn Center near City Hall. This is operated by the Philadelphia Convention and Visitors' Bureau. Its services are free, and it is open every day of the year except Christmas.

Here tourists, convention visitors and Philadelphia residents as well, can obtain accurate and up-to-date information about hotels, motels, restaurants, stores, admission prices and hours for all places of interest.

Philadelphia Tourist Center
Telephone 215-864-1976

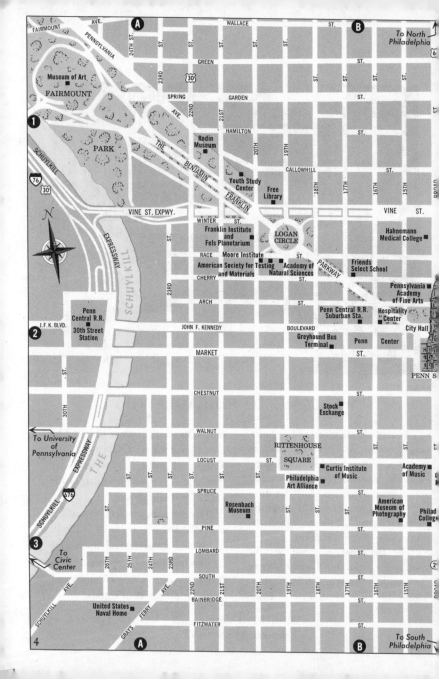

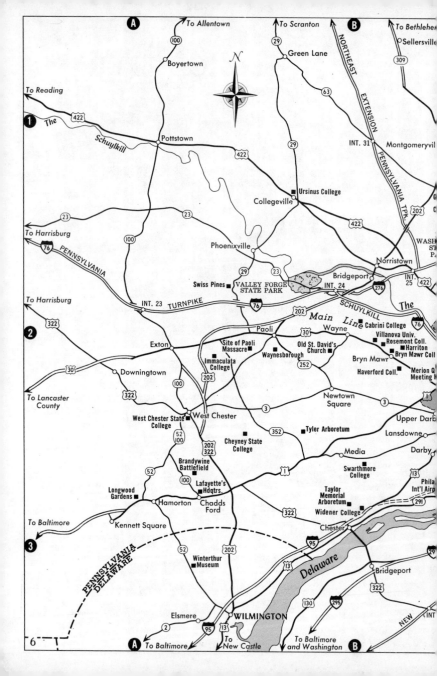

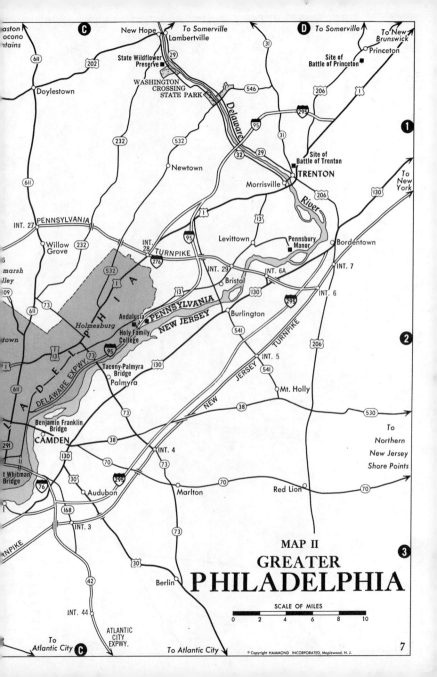

MAP II
GREATER
PHILADELPHIA

SCALE OF MILES

0   2   4   6   8   10

© Copyright HAMMOND INCORPORATED, Maplewood, N. J.

7

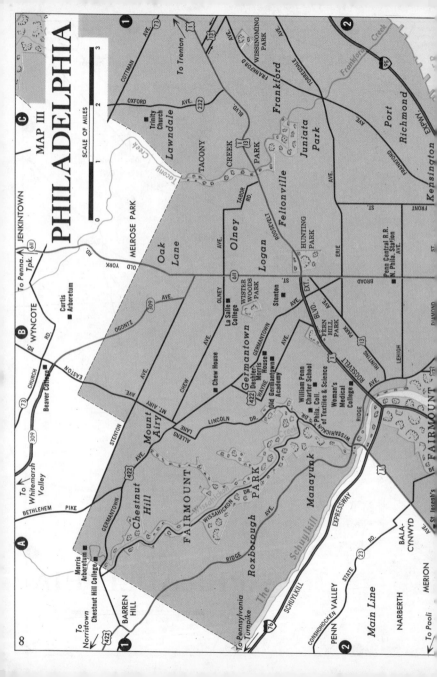

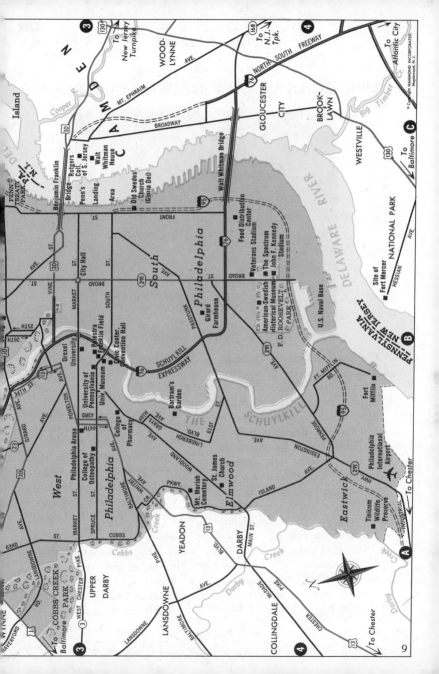

THE QUAKER CITY OF WILLIAM PENN

The most prominent landmark in Philadelphia is the huge statue of the founder, William Penn, on City Hall Tower. (*Map I-B2*)

Penn was born into a wealthy and influential British family in 1644. Early in life he joined the Religious Society of Friends (Quakers) and turned to religious writing and teaching. He served several terms in prison for his beliefs, and he began to plan a colony in the new world where all men could enjoy religious and political freedom.

In 1681, Penn was granted a province in America in settlement of a debt King Charles II owed his father. The King named the province Pennsylvania or "Penn's Woods."

William Penn was an organizer and statesman as well as religious leader. He planned his city and his province in detail. He signed charters granting self-government and religious freedom. He named his capital city Philadelphia meaning "City of Brotherly Love."

Penn's principles were incorporated later in the Declaration of Independence and the Constitution of the United States. Jefferson called Penn "the greatest lawgiver the world has produced."

Pennsylvania was established without war or bloodshed. Penn's belief in human brotherhood guided his dealing with the Indians. His honesty and fairness won their respect.

One of the treasures at the Historical Society of Pennsylvania (*Map I-C3*) is this letter which Penn sent to "the King or Kings of the Indians" before his first visit to America.

London: 18th 8th Mth: 1681

My Friends
  There is one great God and Power that hath made the world and all things therein, to whom you and I and all People owe their being and well being, and to whom you and I must one Day give an account, for all that we Doe in the world; this great God hath written his Law in our hearts by which wee are taught and commanded to Love and help and Doe good to one another and not to Doe Harm and Mischief one unto another * * * *
  I shall shortly come to you myself at what time wee may more Freely and Largely Confer and Discourse of these matters: in the mean time I shall send my Commissioners to treat with you about Land and afirm a League of Peace: Let me Desire you to be kind to them and the People, and Receive those presents and tokens which I have sent to you as a Testimony of my good will to you and my resolution to live justly, peaceably, and Friendly with you.
  I Am your Loving Friend
  Wm Penn

For the King or Kings of the Indians in Pennsylvania

PENN'S WAMPUM BELT

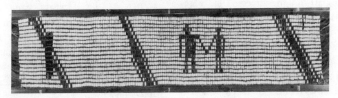

The Indians gave Penn this wampum belt as a token of friendship, the beaded design showing a firm handclasp of red man and white man. It is now in the museum of the Historical Society.

"PENN'S TREATY WITH THE INDIANS"

This painting is known throughout America. The original is in the Pennsylvania Academy of the Fine Arts in Philadelphia. (*Map I-B2*) Although not completely accurate historically, it portrays faithfully the spirit of Penn's government.

The painting is by the Quaker artist, Benjamin West, who was born in 1738 in a house which still stands on the Swarthmore College campus near Philadelphia. (*Map II-B3*) West spent most of his life.

at the British court and was once president of the Royal Academy of Arts in London.

The tree in the painting was known as the "Treaty Elm" and stood for more than a century after Penn's time on the riverfront near a street named Shackamaxon. This is one of many Indian names still used in Penn's city. The elm blew down in 1810, but visitors will find the location marked by a stone monument in Penn Treaty Park. (*Map III-C3*)

PENNSBURY MANOR

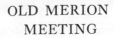

As proprietor and governor of Pennsylvania, Penn lived at this handsome country estate on the Delaware River above his city. (*Map II-D2*)

During Penn's later years in England, Pennsbury fell into disuse and was torn down. The estate has now been restored and furnished under the leadership of the Pennsylvania Historical and Museum Commission.

OLD MERION MEETING

The oldest house of worship still in use in Pennsylvania is the Merion Quaker Meeting House dating back to 1695. (*Map II-B2*) Tradition says that Penn spoke here. Meetings for worship are held every Sunday or "First-day."

SWEDISH SETTLERS PRECEDED PENN

Nearly fifty years before William Penn founded Philadelphia in 1681, Swedish settlers established the colony of New Sweden on the Delaware River. (Dutch colonists came even before the Swedes, but did not leave a permanent settlement.)

Peter Minuit was the first governor of New Sweden. He led the colonists ashore on March 29, 1638 after purchasing land from the Indians. He built Fort Christina near Wilmington. In 1642, the third governor, Johan Printz, moved the capital of New Sweden to Tinicum Island, now in Pennsylvania. The colony flourished for seventeen years, but the rule of the Swedes came to an end when Peter Stuyvesant led a conquering Dutch expedition up the Delaware in 1655. The Dutch in turn were overthrown by the English in 1664.

Not far from Tinicum, in what is now South Philadelphia, is the handsome headquarters building of the American-Swedish Historical Foundation and Museum. Some reminders of the Swedish settlers may be seen in the Philadelphia area including five of their early churches.

American-Swedish Historical Museum (Map III-B4)

The Museum's painting of Peter Minuit establishing New Sweden in 1638.

14

William Penn and the Liberty Bell

The historic Liberty Bell in Independence Hall, Philadelphia, bears a Biblical inscription: "Proclaim liberty throughout all the land . . ."

Few people realize, however, that the great bell and its memorable words originally commemorated the liberty that William Penn granted to the settlers of Pennsylvania. The bell with its prophetic message hung in the tower of the Pennsylvania State House for twenty-five years before American independence was born.

Penn had granted a charter of liberties and privileges to his province in 1701. On the fiftieth anniversary of that charter in 1751, the Pennsylvania Assembly ordered a commemorative bell. A particularly appropriate Biblical verse, Leviticus 25:10, was chosen. It begins "And ye shall hallow the fiftieth year, and proclaim liberty through-out all the land unto all the inhabitants thereof . . ."

The message of freedom was already inscribed on the bell when, in 1776, it was rung to proclaim American independence.

Penn's charter of liberties is still preserved in City Hall. (Map I-B2)

WILLIAM PENN'S PLAN OF 1681
IS STILL VISIBLE IN PHILADELPHIA

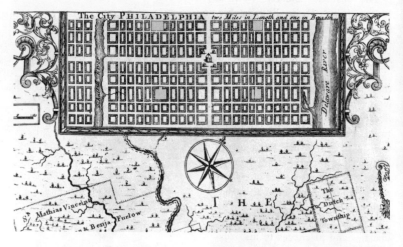

This plan of Philadelphia was made in 1681 by Penn's surveyor, Thomas Holme, whose name is now carried by the section of Philadelphia called Holmesburg. (*Map II-C2*) It is preserved at the Historical Society of Pennsylvania. (*Map I-C3*)

Holme's plan clearly shows Penn's concept of his city as "a greene Country Towne" with straight, treelined streets and well-planned open spaces. There was to be a center square for the "public buildings," and a corresponding open space in the middle of each of the city's quadrants.

Today the city hall stands in the center appropriately named Penn Square. (*Map I-B2*) The other four open spaces still exist in the modern city. In the northwest quadrant is Logan Circle (*Map I-B2*) named for James Logan, one of Pennsylvania's greatest men. (p. 22) In the northeast quadrant is Franklin Square (*Map I-C1*); in the southeast Washington Square (*Map I-C3*); and in the southwest Rittenhouse Square (*Map I-B3*) named for David Rittenhouse, Philadelphia mathematician and scientist.

Rittenhouse Square

Logan Circle

Franklin Square

Washington Square

PHILADELPHIA STILL "THE QUAKER CITY"

Philadelphia Yearly Meeting

For nearly three hundred years Penn's city of Philadelphia has continued to be a center of Quaker thought and activity. Throughout the city and suburbs there are Quaker meeting houses where Meetings for Worship are held weekly and where Meetings for Business are conducted each month.

The first Quaker meeting houses in Philadelphia have long since been replaced. Some of the oldest surviving meeting houses are to be seen in the area surrounding the city, but three colorful places of Quaker worship are still found in the heart of downtown Philadelphia—at 4th and Arch Streets, at 15th and Race Streets, and on 5th and Arch Streets.

At the Arch Street Meeting House Friends still gather as they have for nearly three hundred years for the Philadelphia Yearly Meeting. A number of exhibits relating to Quaker history may be seen.

Philadelphia is the headquarters of the American Friends Service Committee which directs humanitarian projects of many kinds in the United States and abroad. Quaker-founded schools and colleges are numerous throughout the Philadelphia area.

LEADING CITY OF THE COLONIES

Philadelphia was the largest city in Colonial America, and, in sections that have been carefully preserved and restored, much of the charm and beauty of the old city may be seen today. Visitors may walk the same streets, see the same houses and public buildings and worship in the same churches that were here long before the Revolution. On the wall of Old Christ Church a bust of King George II still looks down on his Colonial town.

18th Century tavern now a colorful museum

19

THE POWEL HOUSE

(Map I-D3)

One of the most fashionable houses of Colonial Philadelphia still stands at 244 South Third Street. It was built in 1765 and was the home of Samuel Powel, a wealthy property owner who was mayor of the city in 1776.

Samuel Powel continued to occupy a rear wing of the house during 1777 and 1778 when the mansion was taken over by the British Lord High Commissioner. After the Revolution, Powel was again elected mayor—the first to hold that office under the new government.

The Powels became personal friends of George and Martha Washington. The Washingtons were often entertained in this house, and the Powels in turn visited at Mount Vernon. Washington on occasion occupied the Powel family pew at nearby St. Peter's Church.

In the garden of the Powel House is a pear tree which is as old as the house itself.

ELFRETH'S ALLEY   (*Map I-D2*)

The more modest houses of ordinary working people of Colonial days are also still preserved in Philadelphia. This is Elfreth's Alley—a narrow thoroughfare cut through the middle of one of the larger blocks of streets laid out by William Penn.

This alley dates back to 1700.

Colonial blacksmiths, river pilots, tailors and cabinet-makers resided here. Their original brick houses are still standing—and still lived in—virtually unchanged in appearance for some two hundred years. Over the front door of one house is an open-air spinning wheel gallery.

STENTON—HOME OF JAMES LOGAN (*Map III-B2*)

One of the most influential men in early Pennsylvania was James Logan. As a young man he was secretary to William Penn. In his old age he was friend and adviser to Benjamin Franklin.

For fifty years Logan was agent and representative of the Penn family in America. He held many offices, including president of the provincial council and Chief Justice of Pennsylvania. He was also a successful businessman, making a fortune in fur trading and the iron business.

After he married at the age of forty, Logan bought a tract of five hundred acres of forest land north of Philadelphia and there built Stenton, one of the finest of Phila-

delphia's surviving Colonial mansions. Stenton is now owned by the city of Philadelphia. It is beautifully furnished and maintained by the Society of Colonial Dames of America in the Commonwealth of Pennsylvania.

James Logan was a brilliant scientist and scholar. He knew Greek and Hebrew as well as French and Spanish. He corresponded in Latin with learned men abroad. He collected at Stenton the finest library in the American colonies, and left it at his death to the people of Philadelphia. Called the Loganian Library, his collection of books is still intact and in the possession of the Library Company of Philadelphia (p. 46).

OLD GERMANTOWN

(Map III-B2)

William Penn in 1683 deeded a tract of land northwest of Philadelphia to thirteen families of German settlers led by Francis Daniel Pastorius. They established the community of Germantown which had a long, independent history before being consolidated into the city. Germantown was one of our earliest industrial centers.

Old Germantown Academy—*Built in 1760. George Washington sent his adopted son here. Still in use as a private school.*

Mennonite Meeting House—*Some of the original settlers of Germantown were German Quakers, or Mennonites. They established the first Mennonite Meeting in America in 1683. This building dates back to 1770.*

Rittenhouse Cottage—*Built in 1707 by William Rittenhouse who operated nearby the first paper mill in America. His great-grandson, David Rittenhouse, mathematician and scientist, was born here in 1732.*

Market Square, Germantown—*Laid out in 1703. Here were the market sheds, the firehouse, jail, and stocks of old Germantown. In background at left is the first brick residence in Germantown, now the headquarters of the Germantown Fire Insurance Company.*

Upper Burying Ground—*Some of Germantown's first settlers are buried here. In the background is Concord schoolhouse built in 1775.*

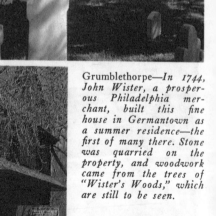

Grumblethorpe—*In 1744, John Wister, a prosperous Philadelphia merchant, built this fine house in Germantown as a summer residence—the first of many there. Stone was quarried on the property, and woodwork came from the trees of "Wister's Woods," which are still to be seen.*

SOCIETY HILL

One of Philadelphia's outstanding urban renewal projects is the restoration of the old Colonial residential area called Society Hill. (The name comes from a land promotion company chartered by Penn and called the Free Society of Traders.)

Here within walking distance of Independence Hall, virtually all buildings have been torn down except those of the Colonial and early Federal period. Old residences are being restored as town houses. Visitors may see a large part of old Philadelphia just as it was before the Revolution. (*Map I-D3*)

HISTORIC SHIPPEN-WISTAR HOUSE   (*Map I-D3*)

Among the most historic residences in old Society Hill is this home built about 1750. At the time of the Revolution it was occupied by Dr. William Shippen, one of the Pennsylvania delegates to the Continental Congress which met just a few blocks from his home.

Dr. Shippen's son, also a physician, was director general of hospitals for the Continental army. The wife of the younger Dr. Shippen was Alice Lee of Stratford Hall, Virginia. When two of her brothers came to the Continental Congress as delegates from Virginia they stayed in this house and it became the center of the cause of Independence.

Twenty years later, this same house became the home of another great Philadelphia physician, Dr. Caspar Wistar, who was a president of the American Philosophical Society. The wistaria vine is named for him. A scholar and a genial host, he began the evening gatherings called "Wistar Parties" which are still held in Philadelphia.

This house is now occupied by the Mutual Assurance Company for Insuring Houses from Loss by Fire. It was founded in 1784 and its emblem or fire mark is the "Green Tree" which is seen on many Philadelphia buildings.

JOHN BARTRAM'S GARDEN

(Map III-B3)

This is the home of another famous Philadelphian of the Colonial era, John Bartram, the botanist. A farm boy, largely self-taught, he became the correspondent and friend of prominent people in Europe and America. He traveled throughout the colonies, collecting trees and plants for his small plantation along the Schuylkill.

In the midst of Bartram's garden there still stands the sturdy stone house originally built by Swedish settlers. Bartram added to it in 1729 and again in 1770. He carved in a stone beneath one of its windows a statement of his faith: "It is God alone, Almyty Lord The Holy One by Me Ador'd."

THE COLONIAL CHURCHES

Old Swedes' Church, *Delaware Avenue near Christian Street*

GLORIA DEI (OLD SWEDES') CHURCH   (*Map III-C3*)

The oldest surviving Colonial church within city limits of modern Philadelphia is Gloria Dei or Old Swedes' Church, a memento of the early Swedish settlements along the Delaware. On this site in 1677 the Swedes built a log church whose walls were provided with loopholes for defense.

In 1698 the present church was begun on the same site. It was dedicated in 1700 and later English settlers called it "a cathedral in the forest." Today it is an island of quiet and charm in the busy port area of modern Philadelphia.

The church's original font is located close to the altar. The vestry contains rare Bibles and historic relics. On the front of the organ gallery are two historic items brought from Sweden by early settlers—a carving of two wide-eyed cherubs and an opened Bible with Christmas quotations in Swedish.

Old Swedes' Church has been declared a national historic site. It serves an active Episcopal parish with services every Sunday.

OLD ST. JOSEPH'S CHURCH
(*Map I-D3*)

Penn's Charter guaranteeing religious liberty attracted colonists of many faiths to his city. St. Joseph's Roman Catholic Church was established in 1733 at a time when Catholic worship was prohibited by law everywhere else in Britain and in America. The original church has been rebuilt twice, but the entryway from narrow Willing's Alley still retains its Colonial atmosphere.

WHEN IN 1733
ST. JOSEPH'S ROMAN CATHOLIC CHURCH
WAS FOUNDED AND
DEDICATED TO THE GUARDIAN OF THE HOLY FAMILY
IT WAS THE ONLY PLACE
IN THE ENTIRE ENGLISH SPEAKING WORLD
WHERE PUBLIC CELEBRATION OF
THE HOLY SACRIFICE OF THE MASS
WAS PERMITTED BY LAW

IN 1734
THE PROVINCIAL COUNCIL OF PENNSYLVANIA
DEFENDING THE LIBERTY OF WORSHIP
GRANTED BY WILLIAM PENN TO THIS COLONY
SUCCESSFULLY WITHSTOOD
THE DEMAND OF THE GOVERNOR OF THE PROVINCE
THAT THIS CHURCH BE OUTLAWED
AND SUCH LIBERTY BE SUPPRESSED

THUS WAS ESTABLISHED PERMANENTLY
IN OUR NATION
THE PRINCIPLE OF RELIGIOUS FREEDOM
WHICH WAS LATER EMBODIED INTO
THE CONSTITUTION
OF
THE UNITED STATES OF AMERICA

MIKVEH ISRAEL (*Map I-C3*)

The Penn family granted the land used for the burial ground of Philadelphia's first Jewish community, the Congregation Mikveh Israel. Surrounded by a brick wall, the graveyard appears now as it did in Colonial days, and contains the grave of the patriot Haym Salomon.

Old Pine Street Church (*Map I-D3*)— *The only Presbyterian Church in Philadelphia preserved from the Colonial period. First services held in 1768. During the Revolution the church was used by the British as a hospital.*

Old St. George's Church (*Map I-D1*)—*First Methodist Church in America. Its services date back to 1769.*

CHRIST CHURCH   *Second Street, North of Market (Map I-D2)*

Silver Pieces Presented by Queen Anne

1744 Chandelier

Christ Church was organized in 1695 and is generally regarded as the most historic of Philadelphia's Colonial churches. The present building, begun in 1727, is an outstanding example of the best in Colonial architecture.

The church tower and spire were added in 1754, financed by a lottery of which Benjamin Franklin was one of the managers.

Franklin's family had a pew in Christ Church, as did Washington. Seven signers of the Declaration of Independence are buried in the burial grounds: Franklin, Joseph Hewes, Francis Hopkinson, Robert Morris, George Ross, Benjamin Rush, and James Wilson.

Bishop White House—*For 64 years, from 1772 until 1836, the minister at Christ Church was Dr. William White, who became bishop in 1787. His home at 309 Walnut Street is now part of Independence National Historical Park and open to visitors by appointment. (Map I-D2)*

ST. PETER'S CHURCH
(*Map I-D3*).

In old St. Peter's Episcopal Church whose tall and graceful spire dominates the now-restored Society Hill area, visitors will see the original high box pews (1761).

Number 41 was that of Samuel Powel (see page 20) with whom George Washington sometimes worshipped.

ST. MARY'S CHURCH (*Map I-D3*)

The principal Roman Catholic Church at the time of the Revolution was St. Mary's, founded in 1763. The church itself has been rebuilt, but the old graveyard surrounding it remains unchanged.

THE COUNTRY MANSIONS

LEMON HILL (*Map IV-C4*)

Among Philadelphia's historic treasures are numerous country mansions and estates preserved intact from Colonial days. Half-a-dozen of these, authentically furnished, are located in Fairmount Park, and are open to visitors on tours arranged through the Philadelphia Museum of Art.

One of the best known is Lemon Hill. This was built by a wealthy merchant, Henry Platt, on an estate named "The Hills" long owned by Philadelphia's "Financier of the Revolution," Robert Morris. In its greenhouse, Morris raised the lemon trees which give the mansion its present name.

Oval Parlor at Lemon Hill

Like several other old mansions in Fairmount Park, Lemon Hill is situated within ten minutes of downtown, modern Philadelphia.

35

WOODFORD MANSION   (*Map IV-C3*)

This was the home of William Coleman, merchant, lawyer, judge, and friend of Benjamin Franklin. Franklin said of Coleman that he had "the coolest, clearest head, and best heart, and the exactest morals of almost any man I ever met with." Coleman acquired the

This drawing room in Woodford Mansion has been called by some authorities the loveliest in Colonial America.

property in 1756 and enlarged an earlier house. Later the King's collector of the port and the Crown agent, David Franks, lived here.

Woodford now houses the superb Naomi Wood collection of Colonial furniture and "household gear."

37

BELMONT MANSION   (*Map IV-A3*)

One of the most attractive of the country estates near Colonial Philadelphia was Belmont, built by William Peters on a broad plateau overlooking the Schuylkill. It bears a date stone, 1745.

Richard Peters, a son who lived here, was Commissioner of War during the Revolution and was later appointed a Federal judge by President George Washington.

Now in the midst of Philadelphia's Fairmount Park, Belmont Mansion is one of the favorite spots of the city's own residents. Its broad lawns afford a magnificent view of the downtown skyline. An open-air restaurant is operated there in summer months, and adjoining the Mansion is the popular Playhouse in the Park.

SWEETBRIER

(Map IV-B4)

This fine house was the home of Samuel Breck. It was built in 1797. In its beautiful south parlor Breck entertained many distinguished guests, both American and French. Breck wrote the delightful book "Recollections" which gives an entertaining picture of his life and times.

STRAWBERRY MANSION   (*Map IV-B2*)

The first house on this site was owned by Charles Thomson, secretary of the Continental Congress. It was burned by British troops searching for Congressional records. The present mansion was started in 1797 by Judge William Lewis. It gets its name from exceptionally fine strawberry plants imported and cultivated by one of the early occupants. Pictured above is the handsome music room.

MOUNT PLEASANT
(*Map IV-B3*)

John Macpherson, a Scottish sea captain who made a fortune in privateering, built this mansion in 1761-62. It was called "the most elegant country seat in Pennsylvania" by John Adams when he visited in 1775. During the Revolution it was the residence of the Spanish minister. Benedict Arnold purchased it but never occupied it. (p. 79) The room shown below is the second-floor "great chamber."

CITY OF BENJAMIN FRANKLIN

Franklin Memorial at Franklin Institute, Philadelphia   (*Map I-A2*)

Benjamin Franklin's Memorial is not in Washington but in Philadelphia at the Franklin Institute on the Benjamin Franklin Parkway. (*Map I-A2*)

Born in Boston, Franklin came to Philadelphia at 17 as a poor young man. He was a printer's apprentice until he started his own print shop at 22. In twenty years he had earned a fortune, then lived another forty years to become philosopher, scientist, public servant, statesman, and the best-known American of his time.

Half a dozen organizations founded by Franklin still flourish today. And some of Franklin's money is still held in trust under his will for the benefit of the City of Philadelphia. Part of the trust was used to help build Franklin Institute. The remainder will be distributed in 1990, the 200th anniversary of Franklin's death.

FRANKLIN
AS A
YOUNG MAN

Franklin's first arrival in Philadelphia as a tired, hungry, and poor young man is well portrayed by this statue on the campus of the University of Pennsylvania (*Map III-B3*), one of the institutions Franklin founded.

A treasure of Franklin's youth was a book *Logic, or the Art of Thinking,* which he read when he was about sixteen. It guided him throughout his life. He presented his copy of the book to the library which he founded. It is still in the possession of the Library Company, along with other Franklin volumes.

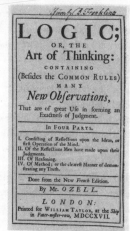

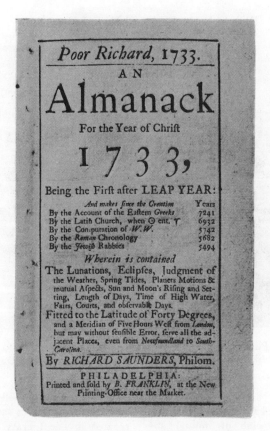

Poor Richard, 1733.

AN

Almanack

For the Year of Chrift

I 7 3 3,

Being the Firft after LEAP YEAR:

And makes fince the Creation	Years
By the Account of the Eaftern *Greeks*	7241
By the Latin Church, when ☉ ent. ♈	6932
By the Computation of *W. W.*	5742
By the *Roman* Chronology	5682
By the *Jewifh* Rabbies	5494

Wherein is contained

The Lunations, Eclipfes, Judgment of the Weather, Spring Tides, Planets Motions & mutual Afpects, Sun and Moon's Rifing and Setting, Length of Days, Time of High Water, Fairs, Courts, and obfervable Days.

Fitted to the Latitude of Forty Degrees, and a Meridian of Five Hours Weft from *London*, but may without fenfible Error, ferve all the adjacent Places, even from *Newfoundland* to *South-Carolina*.

By *RICHARD SAUNDERS*, Philom.

PHILADELPHIA:
Printed and fold by *B. FRANKLIN*, at the New Printing-Office near the Market.

As a printer, the young Franklin was industrious. He published pamphlets and books. He purchased a run-down newspaper, the *Pennsylvania Gazette,* and built it into the largest in the colonies. His greatest financial success was as publisher of *Poor Richard's Almanack*. This is the title page of the first issue published late in 1732 for the year 1733. Only one copy of the first printing is known to be in existence. It is available to scholars at the Rosenbach Museum, Philadelphia. (*Map I-A3*)

BENJAMIN FRANKLIN'S LIBRARY

American Philosophical Society Library—*Modeled after the original building of Benjamin Franklin's Library Company.* (*Map I-D2*)

At the age of twenty-one, Franklin and a group of his friends formed "a club of mutual improvement" for purposes of writing and discussion. It was called the Junto. Four years later, in 1731, Franklin proposed formation of a library and persuaded fifty friends, many of them Junto members, to pool their contributions for purchase of books in England.

The library imported its first books in 1732. It was later incorporated as The Library Company of Philadelphia, and is still in existence. At its headquarters may be seen some of the early minutes written by Franklin as secretary, and the original metal box in which members deposited requests for books to be imported.

The year before Franklin's

death, the Library Company built a handsome brick building across 5th Street from the State House. The original structure was demolished in the 1880's but in recent years the Franklin-founded American Philosophical Society has built its own library on the same site and in the same architectural style. (*Map I-D2*)

The Library Company now occupies a new building at 1314 Locust Street, next door to the Pennsylvania Historical Society.

One of the Library's historical treasures is a huge bust of the "Goddess Minerva as the Patroness of American Liberty." This was the first American "Statue of Liberty." It stood behind the Speaker's desk in the House of Representatives in Congress Hall during the first Congress, and was presented to the Library when Congress moved to Washington. Franklin's Company had served as the first "Library of Congress."

The First Statue of Liberty.

47

AMERICAN PHILOSOPHICAL SOCIETY *(Map I-D2)*

Philosophical Hall is the only private building in Independence Square. It is the headquarters of "The American Philosophical Society, held at Philadelphia, for Promoting Useful Knowledge." The Society was founded by Franklin in 1743 and for two centuries has played an important role in the cultural life of the country.

Franklin was thirty-seven and his printing business was flourishing when he proposed "That One Society be formed of Virtuosi or ingenious Men residing in the several Colonies to be called 'The American Philosophical Society' who are to maintain a constant Correspondence." Franklin served as president throughout the last twenty years of his life, during which time Philosophical Hall was built. The American Philosophical Society not only is still active, but also is the repository of many historic documents and treasures.

Across 5th Street from Philosophical Hall is the new Library building which so nearly duplicates the original home of Franklin's Library Company. It contains an extensive collection of Franklin manuscripts and books.

FRANKLIN'S HOSPITAL
(*Map I-C3*)

Franklin was instrumental in the founding of Pennsylvania Hospital in Philadelphia in 1751. It was the first hospital in America and is still flourishing.

Dr. Thomas Bond conceived the idea of the hospital, and appealed to Franklin for help in financing it. Franklin gave generously himself; he organized a group of contributors; and he worked out a unique arrangement for a matching appropriation from the Provincial Assembly. Franklin was first clerk or secretary of the board of managers, and he was the author of the engaging inscription carved on the hospital cornerstone.

IN THE YEAR OF CHRIST
1755
GEORGE THE SECOND HAPPILY REIGNING;
(FOR HE SOUGHT THE HAPPINESS OF HIS PEOPLE)
PHILADELPHIA FLOURISHING,
(FOR ITS INHABITANTS WERE PUBLICK-SPIRITED)
THIS BUILDING,
BY THE BOUNTY OF THE GOVERNMENT,
AND OF MANY PRIVATE PERSONS
WAS PIOUSLY FOUNDED,
FOR THE RELIEF OF THE SICK AND MISERABLE.
MAY THE GOD OF MERCIES
BLESS THE UNDERTAKING!

Pennsylvania Hospital still occupies its original site and uses—along with other buildings—the original hospital structure which appears today much as it did more than two hundred years ago. Pennsylvania Hospital has been the scene of numerous "firsts" in American medicine.

49

FRANKLIN'S FIRE INSURANCE COMPANY

Franklin was one of the directors who helped found, in 1752, what is now the oldest insurance company in America. He published its notices in his newspaper and printed its policies in his printshop. The company is the Philadelphia Contributionship for the Insurance of Houses From Loss by Fire. (*Map I-D3*) The company is also called "Hand-in-Hand" from its old fire mark which may still be seen on many houses in Philadelphia and suburbs. Today the company is housed in a handsome old building on 4th Street where visitors may sign the register with a quill pen and may see the parchment scroll signed by its early policyholders. Franklin's name heads the list.

FRANKLIN'S HOME

In his later years Benjamin Franklin lived in a handsome house situated in a courtyard and reached through an archway on the south side of Market Street between 3rd and 4th Streets. About twenty years after Franklin's death this building was torn down. This is an artist's concept of how it looked.

FRANKLIN'S BOOKS

Franklin's extensive library was scattered after his death. Many books, however, have been acquired over the years by the American Philosophical Society and are now housed in this room in the Society's library.

Franklin Court is included in Independence National Historical Park. After much archeological digging and historical research, an interesting Franklin exhibit has been arranged.

FRANKLIN'S UNIVERSITY

(Map III-B3)

Benjamin Franklin was also the founder of the University of Pennsylvania. His *Proposals relating to the Education of Youth in Pennsylvania* provided the necessary impetus which transformed the "Charity School," established in 1740, into the "College, and Academy, and Charitable School of Philadelphia."

Franklin was first president of the trustees of the academy which became the University of Pennsylvania in 1791.

Since 1872 the university campus has been located in West Philadel-

Academy Bell—At one time this bell rang for both the Academy and the Union Fire Company, which Franklin founded and which was located nearby. The bell is now on exhibition at the University library.

phia. One of the city's great urban redevelopment programs is now centered around this area.

The athletic stadium at the university is named Franklin Field in honor of the founder.

LIFELONG
PUBLIC
SERVANT

Night Watchman's Box

Franklin devoted himself to public service throughout his life. He served as Philadelphia alderman and city councilman. He organized a night watch to protect citizens and their homes. He drew up the first plan for paving the city streets.

Franklin was clerk and later a member of the Pennsylvania Assembly for many years. He was postmaster for the province and, afterwards, for all of America. He spent some fifteen years in England as agent for Pennsylvania.

In contrast to the many young men of the American Revolution, Franklin was seventy years old when he served in the Continental Congress and as a member of the Committee of Five which drafted the Declaration of Independence. He went to Paris as agent of Congress and negotiated the all-important alliance with France. Later he was minister to France.

At the age of eighty-one Franklin was the elder statesman of the Constitutional Convention. He was the author of the principal compromise which led to the adoption of the Constitution. Finally, he was elected to three terms as president of the executive council of Pennsylvania, retiring just before he died at age eighty-four.

53

BENJAMIN FRANKLIN'S GRAVE

When Franklin died in 1790, he was buried in the burial ground of old Christ Church. This graveyard was located at what was then the

edge of the city at 5th and Arch Streets. The stone slab marking the resting place of the statesman and his wife bears a plain inscription exactly as written out by Franklin himself in his will. The will itself, in which Franklin identifies himself first as a printer and then as government official, is preserved in the library of the American Philosophical Society, which he founded. In recent years it has been customary for visitors to Franklin's grave to place pennies on it out of respect and affection for "Poor Richard."

CITY OF INDEPENDENCE

As tension developed between the American colonies and Great Britain, Philadelphia became a focal point of organized opposition to British colonial policy.

The city successfully defied the Stamp Act passed by Parliament in 1765. When the ship *Royal Charlotte* brought the first stamps and stamped paper to Philadelphia, a mass meeting was held in the Pennsylvania State House; the resignation of the stamp commissioner was demanded; merchants resolved to import no more English goods until the tax was repealed; and newspapers announced they would suspend publication rather than submit to the tax.

The stamps intended for Philadelphia were never used. They went back to England on the same ship which brought them. At the Library Company of Philadelphia (*Map I-B3*) this issue of the *Pennsylvania Journal* for October 31, 1765 tells the story of Philadelphia resistance.

THE PHILADELPHIA TEA PARTY

Philadelphia also led opposition to the British tax on tea, holding a "Tea Party" that was less spectacular than, but just as effective as, the one in Boston.

In September, 1773, word was received in America that the first tea shipments were on their way. Philadelphians held a town meeting at the State House on October 17 and adopted eight resolutions. One declared: "that the duty imposed by Parliament upon tea landed in America is a tax on the Americans, or levying contributions on them without their consent."

In Boston three weeks later, a meeting in Faneuil Hall resolved: "the sense of this town cannot be better expressed, than in the words of certain judicious resolves, lately entered into by our worthy brethren the citizens of Philadelphia."

The tea shipment for Boston was the first to arrive, and the cargo was dumped into the harbor there on December 16. On Christmas Day, the ship *Polly* bound for Philadelphia arrived in the Delaware River. Pilots stopped her at Gloucester, New Jersey, below the city, and her master, Captain Ayres, was escorted overland to Philadelphia by a citizens committee. On December 27 he was taken to attend a mass meeting of 8000 Philadelphians in the State House yard. It was the largest crowd ever assembled in the colonies. A number of resolutions were adopted, the first being "that the tea . . . shall not be landed."

The crowd was orderly, but determined. Captain Ayres was convinced. He agreed to sail his ship back home, was given two days to provision her, and then returned to England without any of his cargo being unloaded.

The *Polly* carried, in addition to its cargo of tea, a new bell cast in England for the tower of old Germantown Academy. The bell went back across the ocean with the rest of the unloaded cargo. It was delivered years later, and now hangs in the Academy tower. The British crown may be seen on the tower. (*Map III-B2*)

CARPENTERS' HALL

(*Map I-D2*)

Sentiment for "a Congress of Delegates from all the colonies" came to a head in 1774 after the British had closed the port of Boston, and on September 5, 1774 the First Continental Congress assembled in Philadelphia.

(The courier who rode from Boston to Philadelphia with news of the port's closing was Paul Revere. He also had made the same long journey by horseback to carry word of the Boston tea party.)

When delegates to the Congress arrived in Philadelphia, this handsome building had just been completed by the Carpenters' Company to serve as its headquarters. The delegates were invited to meet here and chose to do so, rather than in the Pennsylvania State House a block away. In the nation's early days, many historic organizations used space in this building.

Carpenters' Hall still stands in Independence National Historical Park. The Carpenters' Company, which was an organization of Colonial builders and master craftsmen, continues in existence and holds meetings in Carpenters' Hall.

Near Carpenters' Hall, two buildings of early Philadelphia, New Hall and Pemberton House, have been reconstructed to house the Marine Corps Memorial Museum and the Army-Navy Museum.

FIRST CONTINENTAL CONGRESS

The delegates to the First Continental Congress were men of ability and prominence in their respective colonies. George Washington and John Adams were among them, but at that time were not as widely known as two of their colleagues, Samuel Adams and Patrick Henry. Benjamin Franklin was in England, in 1774, as agent for the Pennsylvania Assembly and did not attend. Peyton Randolph, leader of the Virginia delegation, was chosen president of the Congress.

Despite their variety of religious affiliations, the delegates invited a clergyman from Christ Church, Jacob Duché, to offer the first prayer. A print of this scene is in the collection of the Independence National Historical Park. Duché was later elected chaplain of Congress.

As its secretary, the Congress chose a Philadelphian, Charles Thomson, a remarkable man who played an important part in the Revolution but is not at all well-known in American history.

At first, the Congress considered a Plan of Union setting up an American legislature to exercise joint control with Parliament. This was voted down. The Congress then adopted a Declaration of Rights and Grievances, written by delegate John Dickinson, a Philadelphia lawyer. It also adopted the Association, pledging colonists not to use British goods nor to trade with Britain until their rights were recognized.

The Congress adjourned on October 26, 1774. It resolved that another Congress should be held in Philadelphia the next May "unless the redress of grievances, which we have desired, be obtained before that time."

THE SECRETARY OF CONGRESS

Charles Thomson of Philadelphia, secretary of the Continental Congress, was a forty-five-year-old former schoolmaster turned businessman. He was not a delegate, but as a member of the Pennsylvania Assembly had helped make arrangements for the Congress. He continued to serve as secretary throughout the Revolutionary period.

Thomson lived first in a fine home overlooking the Schuylkill. (p. 40) After retirement from

public life, he occupied the estate which had been Mrs. Thomson's family home. This had been built in 1704 in the "Welsh Tract" laid out by William Penn. The original name of the estate was "Bryn Mawr" (from which the present Main Line community takes its name). The place later was renamed "Harriton." The house is still standing. (*Map II-B2*)

Independence Hall (The Pennsylvania State House)   (*Map I-D2*)

SECOND CONTINENTAL CONGRESS

The Second Continental Congress met in Philadelphia on May 10, 1775, and sat in the meeting room of the provincial assembly in the Pennsylvania State House—now known as Independence Hall.

There had already been fighting between minutemen and British redcoats at Lexington and Concord in April. Large numbers of militiamen had gathered around Boston. Although Congress sent a conciliatory address to the King, it proceeded to organize the American Continental Army and in June named the Virginia delegate, George Washington, to take charge. He proceeded to Massachusetts and took command at Cambridge.

Toward the end of 1775, Congress established the Navy and the Marine Corps. Esek Hopkins, of Rhode Island, was first commodore of the Navy. One of the captains was a youthful Philadelphia shipmaster, John Barry, who brought into the city in April, 1776, the first captured British vessel. He is sometimes called "the Father of the United States Navy." His statue stands in the center of Independence Square. One of the Navy's first lieutenants was John Paul Jones, hero of daring exploits, whose grave is at Annapolis.

The first commandant of the Marines was a young Philadelphian, Samuel Nicholas. He set up his headquarters in Tun Tavern (*Map I-D2*) near the waterfront.

A RESOLUTION FOR INDEPENDENCE

By 1776, the demand for independence was swelling throughout the colonies. The pamphlet "Common Sense" written by the Philadelphia editor, Thomas Paine, played an important part. In April, North Carolina authorized its delegates in Congress to vote for independence, and in May, the Virginia delegation was so instructed.

On June 7, Richard Henry Lee of Virginia, offered a resolution: "that these United colonies are, and of right ought to be, free and independent States . . ." There were two days of discussion; Congress postponed action for three weeks—until July 1—". . . and in the meanwhile, that no time be lost, in case the Congress agree thereto, a committee be appointed to prepare a declaration."

61

THE DECLARATION OF INDEPENDENCE

Congress named a committee of five to draw up the Declaration of Independence. That group, in turn, entrusted the first draft to thirty-three-year-old Thomas Jefferson of Virginia. While in Philadelphia, he rented rooms in the Graff House on the southwest corner of 7th and Market Streets (*Map I-C2*) and there, during June, 1776, he wrote the most famous of all American documents.

The American Philosophical Society (*Map I-D2*) owns a draft of the Declaration in Jefferson's own handwriting which shows changes in wording suggested by two other members of the drafting committee, Benjamin Franklin and John Adams. The Society also owns a chair in which Jefferson is said to have sat while writing.

The Declaration was completed and reported to Congress on June 28, 1776. On July 1, the delegates resumed consideration of Lee's resolution for independence and adopted it the next day. John Adams wrote that July 2 would go down in history as American Independence Day.

On Thursday, July 4, Congress adopted the Declaration of Independence as a justification for the Resolution of July 2. Congress ordered that the Declaration be printed, and turned at once to other business. There were no ceremonies that day.

On Monday, July 8, the Declaration was proclaimed to a crowd in the State House yard at noon, being read by John Nixon, a member of the Committee of Safety. On July 19, Congress ordered that an official copy be engrossed on parchment, and this copy finally was signed by Congress on August 2, 1776. This signed Declaration is now in the National Archives, Washington, D.C.

Celebration of the Fourth of July as Independence Day began the next year when Congress arranged a dinner for prominent Philadelphians on that date.

Jefferson's Writing Chair

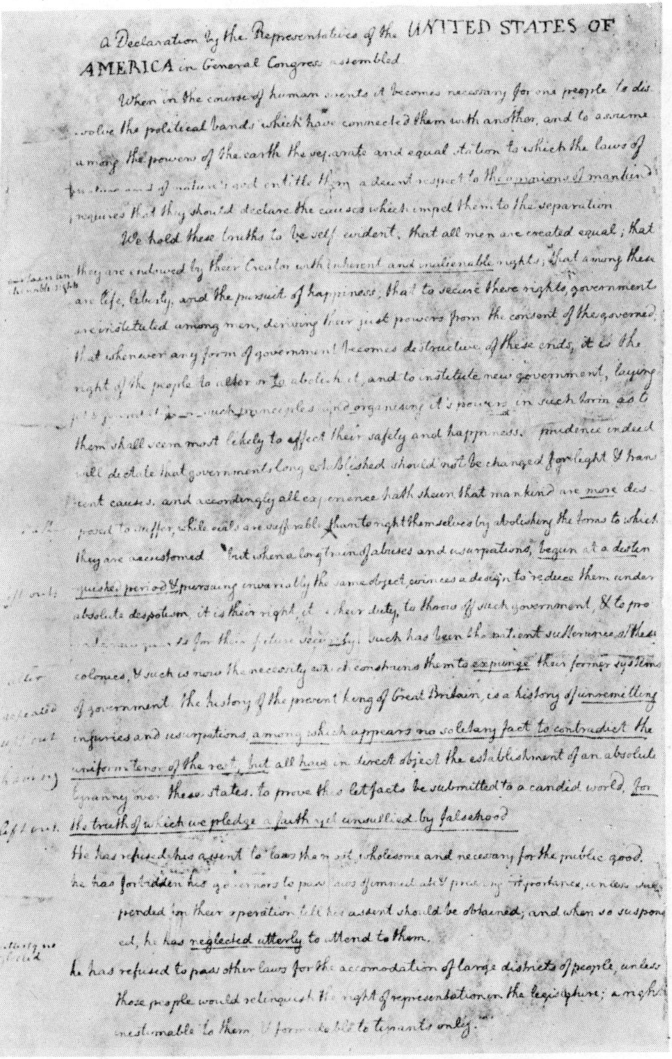

A Declaration by the Representatives of the UNITED STATES OF AMERICA in General Congress assembled.

When in the course of human events it becomes necessary for one people to dissolve the political bands which have connected them with another, and to assume among the powers of the earth the separate and equal station to which the laws of nature and of nature's god entitle them, a decent respect to the opinions of mankind requires that they should declare the causes which impel them to the separation.

We hold these truths to be self evident; that all men are created equal; that they are endowed by their Creator with inherent and inalienable rights; that among these are life, liberty, and the pursuit of happiness; that to secure these rights, governments are instituted among men, deriving their just powers from the consent of the governed; that whenever any form of government becomes destructive of these ends, it is the right of the people to alter or to abolish it, and to institute new government, laying it's foundation on such principles and organising it's powers in such form, as to them shall seem most likely to effect their safety and happiness. prudence indeed will dictate that governments long established should not be changed for light & transient causes: and accordingly all experience hath shewn that mankind are more disposed to suffer, while evils are sufferable, than to right themselves by abolishing the forms to which they are accustomed. but when a long train of abuses and usurpations, begun at a distinguished period & pursuing invariably the same object, evinces a design to reduce them under absolute despotism, it is their right, it is their duty, to throw off such government, & to provide new guards for their future security. such has been the patient sufferance of these colonies; & such is now the necessity which constrains them to expunge their former systems of government. the history of the present king of Great Britain, is a history of unremitting injuries and usurpations, among which appears no solitary fact to contradict the uniform tenor of the rest, but all have in direct object the establishment of an absolute tyranny over these states. to prove this, let facts be submitted to a candid world, for the truth of which we pledge a faith yet unsullied by falsehood.

He has refused his assent to laws the most wholesome and necessary for the public good.

he has forbidden his governors to pass laws of immediate & pressing importance, unless suspended in their operation till his assent should be obtained; and when so suspended, he has neglected utterly to attend to them.

he has refused to pass other laws for the accomodation of large districts of people, unless those people would relinquish the right of representation in the legislature; a right inestimable to them, & formidable to tyrants only.

Draft of the Declaration in Jefferson's Hand

Assembly Room in Independence Hall (*Map I-D2*)

Congress Voting Independence *by Edward Savage*

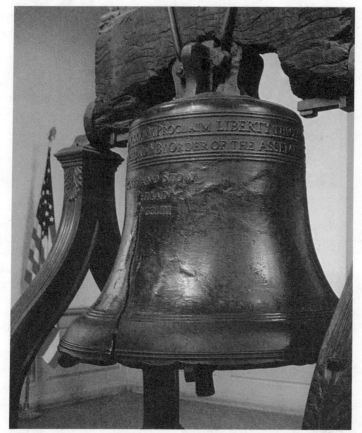

THE LIBERTY BELL

The most venerated symbol of freedom in America is on display at Independence Hall. (*Map I-D2*) It was hanging in the tower of the old building in July, 1776, when Independence was voted and proclaimed. The bell already bore its prophetic inscription: "Proclaim liberty throughout all the land . . ." (p. 15)

65

THE SILVER INKSTAND

In signing the Declaration of Independence, delegates to the Continental Congress used this handsome silver inkstand which the Pennsylvania assembly had purchased for the speaker's table when the State House was first furnished some twenty years earlier. This is now one of the historic treasures at Independence Hall.

EVENING AT INDEPENDENCE HALL

Highlight of a summer visit to Philadelphia for many is an outdoor evening performance in the yard of Independence Hall. Here, on the same ground where the Declaration of Independence was first read to the people, today's visitors can see and hear a stirring presentation of the great events leading to the birth of the nation.

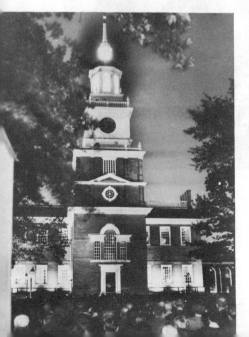

PORTRAIT GALLERY OF THE REVOLUTION

John Hancock
*President of the
Continental Congress
by S. F. B. Morse*

Charles Thomson
*Secretary of the
Continental Congress
by C. W. Peale*

Richard Henry Lee
*Proposer of the
Resolution for Independence
by C. W. Peale*

Thomas Jefferson
*Author of the
Declaration of Independence
by C. W. Peale*

Talented artists came to Philadelphia to earn a living doing portraits of the leaders of the Revolution. One, Charles Willson Peale, filled a museum which he operated in the Long Room of Independence Hall for a quarter century. (p 114)

Some 80 of the Peale portraits and about 100 others are now on permanent exhibit in the Second Bank building in Independence National Historical Park.

WASHINGTON CROSSES THE DELAWARE

By December, 1776, the Continental Army had suffered serious defeats in New York and had retreated across New Jersey into Pennsylvania. British forces appeared to be sweeping triumphantly southward to capture Philadelphia. Congress moved to Baltimore.

Then, on the bitter cold Christmas night of 1776, George Washington and 2400 men recrossed the ice-filled Delaware River from the Pennsylvania side (*Map II-C1*),

surprised the Hessian mercenaries employed by the British, and won the key battles of Trenton and Princeton. (*Map II-D1*) This bold stroke kept Philadelphia safe for the time being, and instilled new life into the Revolutionary effort.

Today there are state parks on both sides of the Delaware at what is known as Washington Crossing. A trip to this historic spot makes a pleasant day's outing for the family visiting Philadelphia.

HOUSE OF DECISION

This double farmhouse near the Delaware River, occupied by the Thompson and Neely families, served in December, 1776 as the headquarters of one of Washington's commanders, General Lord Stirling. Here General Washington held councils of war which led

to the decision to cross the river in open iron ore boats manned by a Massachusetts regiment that included fishermen and seamen from Marblehead.

This house is completely furnished in 18th century style and open to visitors. At the rear is a red cedar tree which was standing at the time of Washington's crossing. Near the house are buried twenty unknown Continental soldiers. Also nearby is the grave of a twenty-four-year-old captain who died of "camp fever" on Christmas Day in the temporary military hospital on the ground floor of the House of Decision.

Seventy-five years after Washington's military feat, this familiar painting was executed by the German-American painter, Emanuel Leutze. The original belongs to the Metropolitan Museum of Art in New York City. A full-size copy in the memorial amphitheatre in Pennsylvania's Washington Crossing State Park is dramatically displayed at the conclusion of an excellent documentary film about the crossing.

POINT OF EMBARKATION

This monument beside the broad Delaware River is near the spot from which Washington and his men embarked on their crossing of the river. Nearby, in the Pennsylvania state park, are an observatory tower overlooking the Delaware Valley, a wild flower preserve with well-marked flower trails, and a large picnic area.

BETSY ROSS AND THE AMERICAN FLAG

On June 14, 1777, the Continental Congress resolved "that the Flag of the United States be thirteen stripes alternate red and white; that the Union be thirteen stars white in a blue field, representing a new constellation."

One of the most popular stories in American history is that a committee of Congress went to the home of the Philadelphia seamstress, Betsy Ross, and engaged her to make the first Stars and Stripes, she showing them with a snip of her scissors how to cut out a five-pointed star. A tiny Colonial house at 239 Arch Street, restored and furnished by patriotic groups, is visited by hundreds of thousands every year as "The Birthplace of Old Glory." (*Map I-D2*)

Not all of the Betsy Ross story can be documented, but there are enough facts to justify persistence of the popular legend. One record in Pennsylvania archives shows a payment on May 29, 1777, to Mrs. Elizabeth Ross "for making ship's Colours etc" for the Pennsylvania Navy. Other records show Betsy Ross made flags for the government for some fifty years after the Revolution. She died in 1836 and is buried in Mount Moriah cemetery, Philadelphia. (*Map III-A4*) The American flag always flies over her grave.

THE BRITISH CAPTURE PHILADELPHIA

Having failed to take Philadelphia in 1776, the British General Howe tried again in 1777. He was unable to force his way up the Delaware River so he sailed up Chesapeake Bay, then marched overland from the south. Washington's army tried to intercept him at Brandywine Creek, near Chadds Ford, Pennsylvania, some thirty-five miles from the city, but the Americans were soundly defeated in the Battle of Brandywine on September 11.

In this battle, the wealthy young French nobleman, Lafayette, was wounded. He had arrived in Philadelphia in July to offer his services. Congress made him a Major General. Another of Washington's generals was the daring "Mad Anthony" Wayne, whose family home, built in 1724, was only a few miles from the battleground. The house, called "Waynesborough," still stands. It contains a number of the general's possessions. (*Map II-B2*)

As the British moved slowly toward Philadelphia, there was sporadic fighting. On September 21 the enemy surprised and routed a small detachment of Wayne's men at night in a bloody engagement which became known as The Paoli Massacre. A park and monument mark the spot along Philadelphia's "Main Line." (*Map II-B2*)

Without further serious fighting, the British entered Philadelphia on September 26, 1777. Their first camp was in the Society Hill area. (*Map I-D3*)

The Continental Congress fled to Lancaster, and then to York, Pennsylvania. The Liberty Bell was taken to Allentown, and hidden beneath the floor of Zion Reformed Church.

Lafayette's Headquarters at Brandywine (Map II-A3)

THE BATTLE OF GERMANTOWN (*Map III-B2*)

Eight days after the British occupied Philadelphia, Washington attempted another surprise attack similar to his crossing of the Delaware the previous year. This resulted in the Battle of Germantown on October 4, 1777.

The British Commander, Howe, had established his quarters at Stenton, the James Logan Mansion. (p. 22) He had posted a three-mile line of troops to protect the city from the north, the line extending through the heart of Germantown. Washington pretended to fortify his camp in Worcester Township, north of Germantown, and then marched his men fourteen miles at night. He divided his force into four columns, each approaching by a different road to surprise the British line at dawn.

The plan was bold and at first successful. The British were thrown into confusion and began a major retreat. Then suddenly, the battle turned into an American defeat when in dense early-morning fog an American officer led his men between two of Washington's columns so that one group of American soldiers was firing upon another.

Washington was forced to order a general retreat. British reinforcements arrived. Howe was able to strengthen and maintain his hold upon the principal city of the colonies.

THE CHEW HOUSE
(*Map III-B1*)

A dramatic incident in the Battle of Germantown centered around Cliveden, the handsome stone house built in 1761 by Benjamin Chew, Chief Justice of the province of Pennsylvania. During the British retreat, a British colonel leading 120 men entered the Chew House and barricaded it.

The first wave of American troops passed by the house and continued in pursuit of the enemy. Later, Washington and his staff arrived on the scene. They halted in front of what is now known as the Billmeyer House, the nearest house to the Chew mansion. Washington surveyed the situation through a field glass, and ordered that the British be dislodged from the Chew House by the American reserve forces.

A young lieutenant from Virginia, carrying a flag of truce, was sent to demand surrender. He was shot and killed as he crossed the

The Chew House Today

lawn. American artillery then began bombarding the house, and several brave men charged the walls in efforts to set the place on fire. The stone mansion withstood all attacks. The Chew House was still in enemy hands when the tide of battle turned into a defeat for Washington. It appears today as it did then.

Chew House During the Battle of Germantown

The Billmeyer House

73

THE BATTLE OF FORT MIFFLIN *(Map III-B4)*

The situation of the British in Philadelphia was at first precarious. Washington's army cut off the flow of supplies by land; the Delaware River was effectively blocked against British ships; food grew scarce; British soldiers burned fences and church pews for firewood; and wounded soldiers and prisoners suffered great hardships.

The river was guarded by a few American warships, by floating gun batteries, and by rows of iron-pointed timbers strung from shore to shore. The most effective defenses, however, were two forts— Fort Mercer on the New Jersey side and what is now known as Fort Mifflin on the Pennsylvania shore.

In order to open a supply route for their bottled-up army, British land and naval forces opened a day-and-night attack on Fort Mifflin on November 10, 1777. The old fort was subjected to intense bombardment. By November 16, it was a ruin, its guns out of action, and 250 men killed or wounded. The defenders did not surrender, however, but successfully evacuated the fort, taking their wounded with them.

Fort Mifflin was rebuilt in 1798 and still stands. Near it may be seen "Cannonball House" a brick

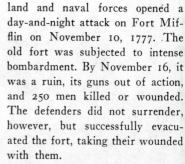

residence built by Swedish settlers as early as 1660. Its walls were pierced by shot during the battle.

The British succeeded in opening the river, and thereafter enjoyed a winter of comfort, sometimes even luxury in Philadelphia while the Continental army suffered in camp.

DAWESFIELD

After the Battle of Germantown, Washington's army remained north of Philadelphia in Whitemarsh Valley (*Map II-C2*), and the general made his headquarters at a number of country houses. For twelve days he was at Dawesfield, built fifty years earlier, and in 1777 the home of James and Elizabeth Dawes Morris. It is still owned and occupied by members of the same family, passing from generation to generation through the distaff side. It is open to visitors by appointment.

Washington established headquarters at Dawesfield on October 21, 1777. Here he and his generals rejoiced over news of the American victory at Saratoga, where the British General Burgoyne surrendered with his entire army. This success enabled Benjamin Franklin, in Paris, to obtain a formal alliance with France.

In the parlor of Dawesfield, a court-martial of General Anthony Wayne was held at his request to investigate charges that he was to blame for the disaster at Paoli. Wayne was acquitted, and the court honored him for bravery.

Washington used one of the upstairs bedrooms of this house. The four-poster in which he slept is still in the room. A first-floor room immediately below this one was used by Lafayette, who could not climb stairs because of a wound suffered at Brandywine.

Washington left Dawesfield on November 2, 1777.

VALLEY FORGE

(*Map II-B2*)

Valley Forge has become a symbol of the hardships endured by American patriots. But this was not a battlefield; it was the camping ground of the cold, ragged, hungry Continental army during the winter of 1777-78 while the British were in Philadelphia.

The once-cheerless hills and fields of Valley Forge are now a state park. A one-day trip to this historic ground should be part of every family's visit to Philadelphia. It is particularly beautiful in spring, with thousands of dogwood trees in bloom.

Washington and his generals made their headquarters in farmhouses and country residences, while other officers and men lived in log huts. Some of the houses remain, and a number of huts have been reproduced.

Adjacent to the park is the Washington Memorial Chapel with its celebrated stained-glass windows and carvings. A stone bell tower houses a carillon which is played at intervals during the day.

Adjoining the chapel is a museum maintained by the Valley Forge Historical Society.

WASHINGTON'S HEADQUARTERS

At Valley Forge, Washington occupied the stone house owned by Isaac Potts, son of the ironmaster of the nearby forge which gave the area its name. The house is now furnished with relics of Washington's occupancy.

It was Potts who later told the story of how one day he came upon Washington's horse tied to a sapling, and in a thicket he saw the General on his knees praying fervently.

There was one great occasion at Valley Forge when news of the alliance with France was received. Washington ordered an entire day of celebration beginning early in the morning with prayer and ending with cannonading and musket fire at night.

Valley Forge Chapel

André, Benedict Arnold and the Philadelphia Tories

The British occupied Philadelphia for nine months. Although many patriot families had fled the city, numerous Tory families remained. They were wealthy for the most part and they entertained British officers lavishly.

One fashionable Tory household was that of Judge Edward Shippen. He and his wife and their daughters frequently had at their home one particular officer, the artistic and talented young John André.

When the British commander Howe resigned and was replaced by General Clinton in May, 1778, Major André arranged an extravagant pageant and ball called "The Meschianza" in Howe's honor.

Ticket to the British Officers' Meschianza

Many Tory young ladies were invited, among them three Edward Shippen daughters. The Meschianza included a regatta, a military procession, a jousting tournament in which British officers and Tory belles played the parts of knights and their ladies, and dancing until 4 A.M. The affair was so elaborate it has been written up at length in Philadelphia histories. Major André conceived and staged the Meschianza; designed costumes and hair styles for the ladies; and painted scenery and decorations.

A month after the Meschianza, on June 18, 1778, the British evacuated Philadelphia. The Americans moved in the same day, and while the main army pursued the British northward, American Gen-

Meschianza Procession

eral Benedict Arnold was made military governor of the city.

Arnold had been a heroic soldier, but a controversial figure. As commander of the city he lived lavishly and preferred the society of the same Tories who had befriended the British. Within a few months, the thirty-seven-year-old Arnold married Judge Shippen's eighteen-year-old daughter, Peggy. He bought an elegant mansion for her (p. 41) but his fortunes were changing, and neither he nor his bride ever lived there.

Arnold was accused of using his military position to enrich himself. Congress ordered him to trial and he was convicted but only reprimanded. Thereafter, he was made American commander at West Point. When he treacherously offered to deliver that fort to the enemy, the British officer designated to negotiate with him was John André, the old friend of Arnold's bride and other Philadelphia Tories.

The conspiracy was discovered. Arnold fled to the British, served for awhile in their army, then went to live in England where his young Philadelphia wife joined him. Major André, however, was captured inside the American lines with evidence in his possession. He was hanged. Just before his death, the talented officer made one more drawing—a sketch of himself awaiting execution.

79

THE END
OF THE WAR

Philadelphia again became the capital of the Revolution after the British withdrew. Congress returned to the assembly room in the State House in July, 1778, and found the building in "a most filthy and sordid situation." It had been used as a barracks, a prison, and a hospital during British occupation.

On July 9, 1778, eight states signed the new Articles of Confederation which finally became effective in 1781.

During the last years of the Revolution, major fighting was in the south. The war ended, for practical purposes, on October 19, 1781 when Washington and the French General Rochambeau trapped Lord Cornwallis and his army on the peninsula at Yorktown while the French fleet held off reinforcements.

Unofficial word of Cornwallis's surrender was brought to Philadelphia by an express-rider who reached the city at 3 A.M. on October 22. A night watchman shouted the news to the populace as he made his rounds. Two days later, Washington's official dispatch was brought by his aide, Colonel Tilghman, a Philadelphian. Congress attended services of thanksgiving at the Dutch Reformed Church and at St. Mary's.

On Saturday, November 3, 1781, twenty-four captured battle flags of Cornwallis's army were brought to Philadelphia, paraded through the streets, and formally presented to Congress at the State House.

THE UNKNOWN SOLDIER OF THE REVOLUTION (*Map I-C3*)

This monument in Washington Square, Philadelphia marks the tomb of the unknown soldier of the Revolution. It is a memorial to all who died to establish American freedom.

Near Washington Square were the city jail, which the British used as a military prison, and the State House, which served both as hospital and as prison. An uncounted number of unfortunate Continental soldiers who died in these buildings were unceremoniously buried in common graves in this Square. No more fitting place could be found for the nation's monument to them.

THE AMERICAN "EMPIRE"

This date stone on the Free Quakers Meeting House at 5th and Arch Streets (*Map I-D2*) illustrates the uncertainty and confusion about the American form of government after the Declaration of Independence in 1776. It refers to 1783 as the eighth year of "the empire."

The Free Quakers Meeting House was built by a group of Friends who organized their own Meeting after they had been disowned by older Meetings for actively supporting the Revolution and serving with Washington in the Continental Army. After the war the Free Quakers rejoined the main body of Friends and the Meeting House was no longer used for religious purposes. Now restored to its original appearance, it is open to visitors during the summer season.

CITY OF THE CONSTITUTION

THE CONSTITUTIONAL CONVENTION

Congress called a Constitutional convention "for the sole and express purpose of revising the Articles of Confederation." But the convention delegates took upon themselves the task of forming a wholly new government.

The convention was to have assembled on May 14, 1787. Delegates were slow to arrive in Philadelphia, however, and it was not until May 25 that meetings began. Washington was unanimously elected president of the convention. There were fifty-five delegates from twelve states (none from Rhode Island). The convention decided its work should be done in private. Only very brief minutes were kept; no one attended the sessions except members. George Washington even discontinued his personal diary for the period of the convention. Historians must trace its proceedings through a few journals, principally one kept by James Madison.

Throughout a hot and humid Philadelphia summer, the delegates met at the State House five and six hours a day, six days a week. They were an able and dis-

James Madison
"Father of the Constitution"

James Wilson
Author of the First Draft

tinguished group of men. Although they had sincere and intense differences of opinion, they reached workable compromises on all important issues. The first draft of the Constitution was written by Philadelphia lawyer James Wilson, and is still preserved at the Historical Society of Pennsylvania. (*Map I-C3*)

On Saturday, September 15, 1787, the convention reached agreement and adjourned over the weekend for the final draft to be printed. Monday, September 17, the delegates met to vote. Benjamin Franklin, ill and feeble at the age of eighty-one, wrote out a fervent appeal for unanimity which was read for him by Wilson. This speech eventually was printed and became the best-known record of the convention.

Franklin's Speech on the Constitution

September 17, 1787

"I confess that there are several parts of this Constitution which I do not at present approve, but I am not sure I shall never approve them; for, having lived long, I have experienced many instances of being obliged by better information or fuller consideration to change opinions, even on important subjects, which I once thought right, but found to be otherwise. It is therefore that the older I grow the more apt I am to doubt my own judgment and to pay more respect to the judgment of others . . .

"I doubt too whether any other convention we can obtain may be able to make a better Constitution. For when you assemble a number of men to have the advantage of their joint wisdom, you inevitably assemble with those men all their prejudices, their passions, their errors of opinion, their local interests, and their selfish views. From such an assembly can a perfect production be expected? It therefore astonishes me, Sir, to find this system approaching so near to perfection as it does . . .

"Thus, I consent, Sir, to this Constitution because I expect no better, and because I am not sure that it is not the best . . . On the whole, Sir, I cannot help expressing a wish that every member of the convention who may still have objections to it would, with me, on this occasion doubt a little of his own infallibility and, to make manifest our unanimity put his name to this instrument."

The completed, official Constitution starts with the familiar Preamble memorized by most Americans in school . . . but the first draft in the hand of James Wilson did not include the Preamble, and designated the new government: "The United People and States of America." At the Historical Society of Pennsylvania. (Map I-C3)

ADOPTION OF THE CONSTITUTION

When debate on the Constitution was concluded, Franklin moved that it be signed as "done in Convention by the unanimous consent of the states present," this language being carefully chosen in view of the fact that Rhode Island was not represented and some individual delegates of other states were not willing to sign. The document was signed by thirty-nine delegates to become effective upon ratification by nine of the states.

Delaware was the first to ratify, thus earning its place as "The First State." Pennsylvania followed five days later, and New Jersey six days after that. The Constitution became effective when the ninth state ratified it on June 21, 1788. Eleven states had approved by the time Washington was inaugurated the first President of the United States on April 30, 1789. The twelfth and thirteenth states ratified the Constitution after the new government had been installed.

THE RISING SUN

While delegates to the convention were signing the completed Constitution on September 17, 1787, according to Madison's journal, the aged Benjamin Franklin called attention to the President's chair which Washington had occupied all through four months of difficult deliberations.

Said Franklin: "I have often and often in the course of the session and the vicissitudes of my hopes and fears as to its issue, looked at that behind the President without being able to tell whether it was rising or setting. But now at length I have the happiness to know that it is a rising and not a setting sun."

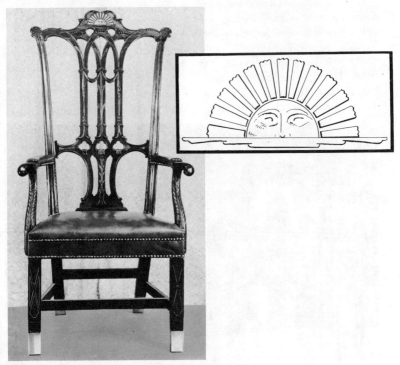

CAPITAL OF THE UNITED STATES

The first capital of the United States under the new Constitution was New York City. However, the First Congress decided that the permanent capital would be a new federal city on the Potomac, and that while the city of Washington was being built, the capital would be Philadelphia.

On December 6, 1790, the First Congress met in Philadelphia, and this continued to be the capital city for the next ten years. At that time, two buildings adjoining the State House had just been completed. The building to the west, at the corner of 6th and Chestnut

Streets, had been built as the Philadelphia County Court House. It was turned over to the Federal Government for the use of Congress, and has been known since as Congress Hall. (*Map I-C2*)

The House of Representatives sat in the large room on the first floor of Congress Hall. The United States Senate met in a room on the second floor. This is where Washington was inaugurated for his second term, and where he delivered his last message to Congress in 1796. (This was not Washington's "Farewell Address," which actually was writ-

ten while Congress was in recess and published in a Philadelphia newspaper, the *Daily Advertiser.* One of Philadelphia's newspapers today is the *Inquirer,* successor to the *Advertiser,* and the oldest daily newspaper in the United States.)

The new building to the east of the State House at 5th and Chestnut Streets (*Map I-D2*) had been intended for use as the Philadelphia City Hall. Here the United States Supreme Court sat.

Philadelphia was still the capital when John Adams, vice-president under Washington, was elected second President of the United States. Adams took the

oath of office in the House of Representatives in Congress Hall, on March 4, 1797. Two years later, Congress assembled there to receive official news of Washington's death at Mount Vernon. The members heard spoken for the first time Henry Lee's famous words "First in war; first in peace; first in the hearts of his countrymen." Lee wrote these words for a funeral oration at Old Zion Lutheran Church. The church was located at 4th and Cherry Streets. (*Map I-D2*) The old building is gone, but the church still exists as St. Michael-Zion German Lutheran Church, Franklin Street above Race. (*Map I-C1*)

THREE PRESIDENTIAL MANSIONS

THE ROBERT MORRIS HOUSE (*Map I-D2*)

While the Constitutional convention was in session, George Washington lived in a house on Market Street west of 5th, owned by his friend Robert Morris. When he returned to Philadelphia as President, he occupied the same house and lived there throughout his term of office. The house has since been demolished, but old drawings of it are in existence and a model may be seen at the Atwater Kent Museum. (*Map I-C2*)

Morris was a wealthy merchant and banker who had helped finance the Revolution. He owned other homes in Philadelphia including the country mansion where Washington was often entertained. (p.35)

THE UNUSED PRESIDENT'S HOUSE (*Map I-C2*)

During Washington's administration, the state of Pennsylvania built a large, imposing President's house on 9th Street between Chestnut and Market. The State legislature apparently hoped this might help keep the national capital at Philadelphia, despite construction of the city of Washington.

The President's house was offered to John Adams when he was inaugurated in 1797, but he declined, saying that Congress would first have to authorize acceptance. Throughout his term, Adams lived in the same Robert Morris mansion on Market Street which Washington had occupied.

THE MANSION IN GERMANTOWN
(*Map III-B2*)

In 1793, a deadly epidemic of yellow fever struck Philadelphia. Many government officials and private citizens fled the city. President Washington rented this house in Germantown from Colonel Isaac Franks and lived here part of the month of November. The President and his family again rented this house in the summer of 1794.

The house is known as the Deshler-Morris House after two of its former owners. Given to the Federal Government, it is now part of the National Historical Park.

The oldest American "White House" still standing, it is furnished in the style of Washington's era and is open to the public.

DOLLEY MADISON'S HOUSE (*Map I-D2*)

The residence at the northeast corner of 4th and Walnut Streets, built in 1776, was purchased in 1791 by John Todd and his wife, Dolley. Todd died in 1793, and the next year his widow married James Madison, then in Philadelphia as a member of Congress from Virginia. When Madison became the fourth President in 1809, Dolley Madison won a wide reputation as White House hostess.

BANK OF THE UNITED STATES

The First Bank
3rd Street,
South of Chestnut
(*Map I-D2*)

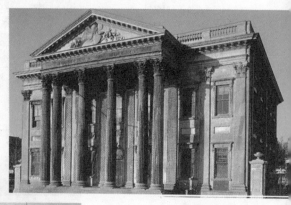

The Second Bank
Chestnut Street,
East of 5th
(*Map I-D2*)

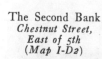

In 1791 Secretary of the Treasury Alexander Hamilton set up a central bank modeled after the Bank of England. This Bank of the United States opened for business in temporary quarters in Carpenters' Hall, then moved into its own building on Third Street near Chestnut.

The Bank was the center of political controversy, and its charter was allowed to expire in 1811. Stephen Girard purchased the building and operated his private bank there until his death. The property was owned by his estate until 1956 when it was incorporated into Independence National Historical Park. It is the oldest surviving bank building in the United States.

In 1816 Congress created a Second Bank of the United States. Philadelphia was still the financial capital of the Nation and this bank's headquarters were built on Chestnut Street near Fifth. It, too, passed out of existence after 20 years. The building served as the Philadelphia Custom House for nearly a century. It now houses Philadelphia's great collection of portraits of the nation's early leaders.

TWO HISTORIC CHURCHES FOUNDED

Mother Bethel Church

Richard Allen's Tomb
in the Church he Founded.

Richard Allen

Two churches organized in Philadelphia during the Nation's earliest days are still active today and are living monuments to two men who were born in slavery but became leaders in their community.

Richard Allen and Absalom Jones established the free African Society in 1787. They were honored by the city for heroic work during the yellow fever epidemic in 1793. Thereafter, each founded a church. Richard Allen purchased property on 6th Street near Pine and in a former blacksmith shop there, organized the African Methodist Episcopal Church. He was the first pastor, and he later became his church's first bishop. The church building, known as "Mother Bethel," still occupies the same site on 6th Street.

Absalom Jones joined the Episcopal Church, established the African Episcopal Church of Saint Thomas, and became its first rector. Later he was ordained priest. The original church was on 5th Street near Walnut. It is now located in West Philadelphia at 52nd and Parrish Streets.

HISTORIC COUNTRY HOUSES

The Highlands

Andalusia

While Philadelphia was the nation's capital, some fine country homes were built to house and entertain leaders of the young nation.

One such mansion is the Highlands, a handsome, stone Georgian house in Whitemarsh Valley, built in 1796 by Anthony Morris who was prominent in the society of the Washington and Adams administrations. In recent years, the Highlands, with its beautiful gardens, has been restored.

Not far away in Whitemarsh Valley (*Map II-C2*) are other celebrated houses of Philadelphia's past. One is Hope Lodge named for members of the Hope banking family of London, who purchased it in 1784. Another is Sandy Run, the Emlen family home, built about 1720. It was one of the houses Washington used as headquarters before Valley Forge. A third historic house is Graeme Park originally built by Sir William Keith, Lieutenant-Governor of Pennsylvania in 1721.

One of the best known country estates of Philadelphia's Federal period is Andalusia on the Delaware River. (*Map II-C2*) It is still occupied as a private residence but is open by appointment. It was built by the Craig family in 1795. Their daughter married Nicholas Biddle, Philadelphia lawyer, diplomat, and banker, who became president of the Second Bank of the United States. One of Biddle's interests was architecture and he was responsible for many of Andalusia's outstanding features, including the Grecian front facing the river. Members of the Biddle family still live here.

(Map I-A3)

(Map I-D2)

PHILADELPHIA'S NAVAL ACADEMY

This imposing marble building occupying a sizable tract of ground at 24th Street and Grays Ferry Avenue, in South Philadelphia, was the predecessor of the United States Naval Academy at Annapolis. It was built in 1830.

In the nation's early days, young midshipmen under instruction on naval receiving ships in Boston, New York, and Norfolk were brought to Philadelphia to attend a naval school here. The building was also used as an "asylum" for retired and disabled men of the Navy and Marine Corps. As the midshipmen's school expanded, it required a separate location and in 1845 it was transferred to Annapolis. This building in Philadelphia still serves as the United States Naval Home.

PHILADELPHIA (MERCHANTS') EXCHANGE

The Philadelphia (Merchants') Exchange built in 1832-1834, an architectural gem of the old city, has been completely restored in appearance by the National Park Service. As a unit of the Independence National Historical Park, it is used for administrative purposes.

CITY OF STEPHEN GIRARD

In June, 1776, the day before Richard Henry Lee offered his resolution for independence in the Continental Congress, a twenty-six-year-old French ship captain named Stephen Girard brought his vessel into Philadelphia to escape British warships. The high seas had become too risky for a profit-minded Frenchman, and Girard had decided to settle down on shore until the trouble blew over.

Girard made Philadelphia his home for the rest of his life. When he died at the age of eighty-one, he was one of the wealthiest men in America, and the greatest benefactor the city has ever had. In modern Philadelphia, the name Girard is commemorated everywhere. A bank, a public school, an important street, and enough business establishments to fill most of a page in the telephone book are all named Girard.

The bulk of Stephen Girard's estate is still held in trust and now amounts to about $99,000,000 It supports Girard College (*Map III-B3*), a school for the care of poor, orphan boys between the ages of six and eighteen.

Despite his wealth, Girard's personal life was unhappy. He was blind in one eye from childhood; his young wife went insane; their only child died in infancy. Girard devoted himself to hard work and to service of his community. During the yellow fever outbreak of 1793, while many wealthy people left the city, Girard personally nursed patients in one of the municipal hospitals.

When the first Bank of the United States passed out of existence in 1811, Girard, who had been a substantial stockholder, acquired the building and established his own private bank there. During the War of 1812, he personally helped finance the United States Government. When the Treasury was able to sell only a small part of a sixteen-million-dollar bond issue, Girard and two other men subscribed for the entire remainder.

Merchant, trader, and banker, Girard was interested in agriculture as well. Almost daily he drove to his farm south of the city. The original farmhouse still remains (*Map III-B4*) and the Girard Estate has built houses on the rest of the land. Girard also owned much other real estate in Philadelphia, and his estate continues to

Founder's Hall, Girard College

The Girard Statue in Founder's Hall

Girard College Campus

Girard College occupies a forty-two acre farm owned by Girard when h[e] died. The institution was formerly north of Philadelphia, but this aerial phot[o] shows how the city has grown around it.

hold most of it, including an entire center-city block from Market to Chestnut Street between 11th and 12th Streets. (*Map I-C2*)

At his death in 1831, Girard left substantial sums of money to improve Philadelphia's waterfront and strengthen its police system. The residue of his estate was left to establish and maintain Girard College. It has about 750 students who live at the school from the time they are admitted until graduation.

Girard's will required that a high wall be built around his school. He also provided that no clergymen should ever be admitted

to the grounds, but this was not because he opposed religion. His will said:

"My desire is, that all the instructors and teachers in the college shall take pains to instil into the minds of the scholars the purest principles of morality, so that, on their entrance into active life, they may, from inclination and habit, evince benevolence towards their fellow creatures, and a love of truth, sobriety and industry, adopting at the same time such religious tenets as their matured reason may enable them to prefer."

Girard's remains are contained in a sarcophagus in Founder's Hall. His private papers, financial records, and many of his personal belongings are preserved in a memorial room in the same building.

MODERN PHILADELPHIA

Downtown Philadelphia At Night—*The city's founder, William Penn, looks down at the modern metropolis from the top of City Hall Tower. Tourists may visit the tower.*

With all its historical background, Philadelphia is also a great modern metropolis. It is a city of vastly diversified industry and commerce; it is a busy seaport; it is widely known as the city of homes; and it is a center of culture, education, and sports. The following pages illustrate for visitors some of the many aspects of modern Philadelphia.

Philadelphia Museum of Art (*Map I-A1*)—*A treasure house of masterpieces of all ages, and one of the leading museums of the world. The building itself is a work of art.*

John F. Kennedy Boulevard (*Map I-A2*)—*In the heart of the city is one of Philadelphia's most modern thoroughfares.*

PENN
CENTER

On the site of what used to be
Philadelphia's old Broad Street
Station and its "Chinese Wall" of
elevated railroad tracks, modern
Penn Center has been created
(*Map I-B2*). This attractive com-
plex of office buildings, plazas, open
concourses and miniature gardens
is regarded by many as the nation's
leading demonstration of urban renewal in the heart of a metropolitan area.

THE PHILADELPHIA ORCHESTRA

Philadelphia is the home of one of the world's finest symphony orchestras. Each year the Philadelphia Orchestra presents about 100 concerts for home town audiences in the city's famed Academy of Music (right). In addition the Orchestra travels widely both throughout the United States and abroad. The Orchestra was established in 1900. The Academy of Music—now owned by the Philadelphia Orchestra Association—is even older, having been built in 1853. As plain on the outside as a brick market place, inside it is a lovely palace of gold and marble with acoustics that music critics say are unsurpassed.

Broad Street and City Hall — *The headquarters of Philadelphia's municipal government is in the huge City Hall in Penn Square at the intersection of Broad and Market Streets. (Map I-B2)*

Robin Hood Dell—*On summer evenings as many as 30,000 persons gather here in Fairmount Park for symphony concerts under the stars. (Map IV-B2)*

PHILADELPHIA—
HOME OF OIC

In 1964 Philadelphia's Rev. Leon H. Sullivan rented an abandoned police station for $1 a year and opened a training center to teach men and women the skills needed to hold jobs in business and industry. He called it the Opportunities Industrialization Center (OIC). Within five years there were five such centers in Philadelphia and a total of seventy throughout the United States.

Members of Dr. Sullivan's Zion Baptist Church formed Zion Investment Associates to establish business ventures which provide jobs for OIC graduates, opportunities for management and business ownership, and profits to be plowed back into additional training centers and business enterprises. Progress Plaza—a new,

modern shopping center on Broad Street—was the first result of this program and became the forerunner of a number of similar centers. It was quickly followed by establishment in Philadelphia of Progress Garment Manufacturing Company and of Progress Aerospace Enterprises, where trained technicians manufacture electronic components for space exploration and for national defense.

OIC and the Progress enterprises are being widely used as models for other self-help undertakings in this country and abroad. They create jobs, income, new opportunity and economic security for those directly engaged in the programs and for their community as well.

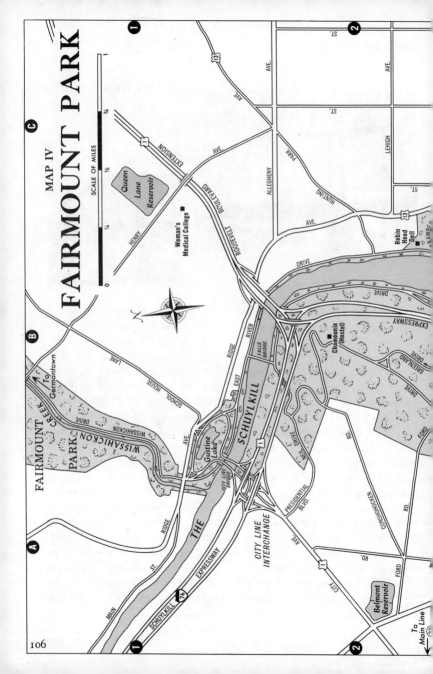

MAP IV

FAIRMOUNT PARK

SCALE OF MILES

0   ¼   ½   ¾   1

Queen Lane Reservoir

Woman's Medical College ■

HENRY

EXTENSION

AVE.

13

AVE.

ST.

ST.

AVE.

ROOSEVELT BOULEVARD

ALLEGHENY AVE.

PARK

HUNTING

LEHIGH

ST.

13

Robin Hood Dell

SCHUYLKILL

FAIRMOUNT PARK

WISSAHICKON

To Germantown

Fairmount Creek

DRIVE

WISSAHICKON DRIVE

SCHOOL HOUSE LANE

RIDGE

AVE.

RIVER

RIDGE

EAST

FALLS BRIDGE

DRIVE

DRIVE

EXPRESSWAY

Chamounix (Hostel) ■

GREENLAND DRIVE

FORD

RD.

Gustine Lake

CITY LINE BRIDGE

THE

SCHUYLKILL

NEILL DRIVE

11

PRESIDENTIAL BLVD.

CITY LINE INTERCHANGE

CONSHOHOCKEN

RD.

MAIN ST.

RIDGE

SCHUYLKILL EXPRESSWAY

76

CITY AVE.

11

FORD RD.

CITY LINE

Belmont Reservoir

To Main Line

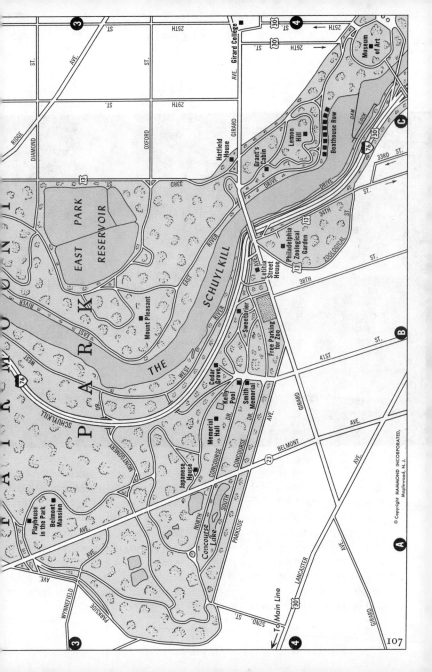

FAIRMOUNT PARK   *(Map IV)*

More than one hundred years ago, farsighted Philadelphians began assembling land for what is now Fairmount Park—more than 4,000 acres along the banks of the Schuylkill and Wissahickon Creek —all owned by the city and maintained as recreation area for its people.

The park is within walking distance of many residential sections of the city. It includes a summer theater, the Zoological Garden, miles of trails for hiking and horseback riding, picnic grounds, and playing fields of all types. It is criss-crossed with scenic roads and highways which provide quick transportation from one part of the city to another.

CONVENTION CITY

Philadelphia is one of the leading convention cities in the United States. Ever since the Continental Congress and the Constitutional Convention met here in the early days of the nation, Americans have been attracted by this city's central location and traditional hospitality.

The largest international trade shows as well as conferences can be housed in Philadelphia's newly expanded and modernized Civic Center. Located on the west bank of the Schuylkill, within a few min-

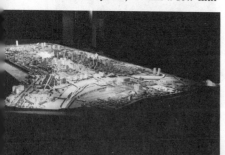

utes of center-city and suburbs, the Civic Center includes several completely air-conditioned exhibition halls, 57 meeting rooms, the Civic Center Museum and a 1000-car garage.

The Civic Center's main auditorium (Convention Hall) seats up to 13,500, and has been the scene of several Presidential nominations as well as opera, ballet, concerts and sports events.

A favorite place for visitors to begin learning about the city is the permanent Philadelphia Panorama exhibit located in the Civic Center Museum, which also features a year-round series of international exhibitions and concerts and regional crafts shows.

STOCK EXCHANGE

Philadelphia's Stock Exchange is the oldest in the nation. It is now housed in a new building at 17th Street and Stock Exchange Place (*Map I-B2*) where there is an attractive visitors' gallery. This is headquarters for the combined Philadelphia - Baltimore - Washington Stock Exchange.

PHILADELPHIA SHOWBOAT

A cruise on the Delaware aboard one of the paddle-wheel Philadelphia Showboats is a good way to see and appreciate the variety of activity in a great seaport. The boats make two-hour cruises morning and afternoon, covering both sides of the river from the Benjamin Franklin Bridge to the Naval Base.

SPORTS COMPLEX

(Map III-B4)

Philadelphia boasts one of the finest groups of sports facilities in the country. Close together in South Philadelphia are Veterans Stadium (baseball and football), The Spectrum (basketball and ice hockey) and the John F. Kennedy Stadium, annually the scene of the Army-Navy football game.

PHILADELPHIA AIRPORT

Philadelphia's International Airport is within city limits at the southwestern edge of town and is connected directly to downtown center-city by high speed expressways. It often handles heavy overseas traffic when New York is fogbound. *(Map III-A4)*

United States Mint (*Map I-D2*)—*Coins have been minted in Philadelphia ever since the birth of the nation. The new United States Mint is located on the new Independence Mall. Here during scheduled hours visitors may have the opportunity to see the manufacture of coins.*

Police Administration Building (*Map I-C2*)—*This handsome new building houses the headquarters of the Philadelphia Police Department. A part of Philadelphia's sweeping downtown development, this building stands on what was once the crime-ridden tenderloin.*

MUSEUMS

Pennsylvania Academy of the Fine Arts—*America's oldest art museum and art school, founded 1805 at a meeting in Independence Hall. One of the leading spirits was the artist Charles Willson Peale. In addition to the Benjamin West painting (p. 12), another famous work owned by the Academy is Peale's portrait of himself and the museum which he maintained in Independence Hall. One block north of City Hall. (Map I-B2)*

Historical Society of Pennsylvania—*Repository of a priceless collection of historical manuscripts, papers, portraits and personal possessions of famous Americans, as well as books and genealogical records. This corner of its museum contains furniture which belonged to Abraham Lincoln.*

AND EXHIBITS

Academy of Natural Sciences
—*America's first natural history museum founded 1812. Most celebrated of its exhibits is this dinosaur nearly two stories high. Logan Circle (Map I-B2)*

Rodin Museum (*Map I-A1*)
—*An impressive collection of Rodin's work is exhibited on the Parkway in a replica of Rodin's museum in France.*

University Museum—*One of the world's leading archaeological museums is the University Museum of the University of Pennsylvania on the campus in West Philadelphia. (Map III-B3) It sponsors archaeological expeditions to many parts of the globe.*

THE PHILADELPHIA ZOO

The Philadelphia Zoological Society maintains in Fairmount Park the oldest zoo in America and one of the finest such institutions in the world, open all year and visited by about one million people annually. One of its attractions is the Children's Zoo where young people may pet ordinary farm animals. The zoo's collection of animals is unusually complete and is displayed with thoughtful imagination. Lawns, trees, and flowers make the zoo truly a zoological garden. (*Map IV-B4*)

Franklin Institute Exhibits—*The science museum at the Franklin Institute features exhibits which visitors may operate, such as a model of a space capsule for moon landings and a full size 350-ton steam locomotive. (Map I-A2)*

Atwater Kent Folk Museum—*This wooden, cigar-store Indian is typical of the exhibits of Americana and of old-time Philadelphia. The museum is housed in the original building of the Franklin Institute erected in 1826. (Map I-C2)*

Philadelphia Maritime Museum—
*Interesting and dramatic exhibits of
the rich maritime heritage of Philadelphia and the nation. (Map I-D2)*

Perelman Antique Toy Museum—
*Unique display of 2000 antique toys
and coin banks. (Map I-D3)*

Fire Museum—*Colorful displays of old
head-drawn and horse-drawn firefighting apparatus housed in a historic
fire house near Elfreth's Alley. It was
formerly the home of a fire company
descended from one Franklin founded.
(Map I, D2)*

THE PORT OF PHILADELPHIA

Nearly three hundred years ago, Penn chose the site of Philadelphia because it is a great natural seaport. The city is in the heart of the greatest marketing area of the nation, a hundred miles from the ocean, yet the largest seagoing vessels can berth at its piers less than a mile from City Hall.

Ship cargoes through the Port of Philadelphia lead the nation in foreign tonnage and exceed all American ports except New York in dollar value. Sightseeing boats provide interesting tours of the harbor in summer months.

Philadelphia was the birthplace of the American Navy and has always been the home of a great naval base (*Map III-B4*) where visitors at scheduled times may go aboard naval warships.

PLACES OF INTEREST NEARBY

While staying in Philadelphia, visitors may easily make one-day trips to many nearby places of interest. For information, ask at the Tourist Center.

Longwood Gardens— *Only 25 miles from central Philadelphia are the renowned Longwood Gardens on the estate of the late Pierre S. du Pont near Kennett Square, Pennsylvania. This photograph shows the Fountain Garden and the Conservatory. The gardens are open to the public without charge. (Map II-A3)*

Henry Francis du Pont Winterthur Museum—*Near Wilmington, Delaware, 25 miles from Philadelphia. Contains over 100 rooms in which are displayed American domestic architecture, furniture, ceramics, metalwork, folk art, textiles, paintings, and prints of the period 1640-1840. Advance reservations required for main museum. Ten rooms in south wing open without appointment. (Map II-A3)*

Other Gardens—*Near Philadelphia are many noted public gardens including the Morris Arboretum in Chestnut Hill; Swiss Pines Park, on Charlestown Road, Valley Forge; Taylor Memorial Arboretum, on Ridley Road, Chester; and the Tyler Arboretum at Lima, Delaware County.*

The Gettysburg Battlefield—*115 miles west of Philadelphia where, after three days of bitter fighting, Confederate General Robert E. Lee's invasion of Pennsylvania was turned back. This is where Abraham Lincoln delivered his immortal Gettysburg Address dedicating "a portion of this hallowed ground" as a national cemetery. Shown above is the field across which General Pickett led his heroic charge against Union forces on Cemetery Ridge.*

Newcastle, Delaware—*Founded even before William Penn planned his Quaker City, in Colonial days this was the capital of Delaware. It still appears much as it did 200 years ago.*

THE COUNTRY—

THE SEASHORE—

THE MOUNTAINS

Philadelphians are fortunate to have country, seashore, and mountains all near enough for a day's visit: the lush and prosperous Pennsylvania Dutch farm country —the beaches and boardwalks of the New Jersey ocean resorts— and the beautiful laurel-covered Pocono Mountains. A drive to see any or all of these can easily be included in every family's visit to Philadelphia.

Lancaster County, Pennsylvania — fifty *miles west of Philadelphia.*

Atlantic City, New Jersey — *sixty-five miles east of Philadelphia.*

The Pocono Mountains—*one hundred miles north of Philadelphia.*

ACKNOWLEDGMENTS

Many individuals and organizations have made generous contributions of information and photographs for use in this book, and the assistance of all is gratefully acknowledged. Much material and many photographs were assembled for the Independence Hall Association by the late Harold D. Eberlein and Cortlandt V. D. Hubbard, and made available by the Association for use in this volume. In addition, particular thanks are due the following: American Philosophical Society · Alfred P. Bramnick · G. Edwin Brumbaugh · Samuel Chew · City of Philadelphia—Office of the City Representative and Director of Commerce · Colonial Philadelphia Historical Society · Estate of Stephen Girard · The Free Library of Philadelphia · The Germantown Historical Society · The Historical Society of Pennsylvania · Independence National Historical Park · Library Company of Philadelphia · Chas. P. Mills and Son Photography, Inc. · Pennsylvania Academy of Fine Arts · Pennsylvania Dutch Tourist Bureau · Pennsylvania Historical and Museum Commission · Philadelphia City Planning Commission · The Philadelphia Convention and Tourist Bureau · Philadelphia Electric Company · Philadelphia Museum of Art · Philadelphia Yearly Meeting of the Religious Society of Friends · The Rosenbach Museum · Martin P. Snyder, Esq. · Alfred J. Wyatt.

INDEX

INDEX